The Key Logger: A Forbidden Glimpse into the True Nature of Women

By Nicholas Jack

Other Books By Nicholas Jack

Elite Online Dating: Read. Click. Bang. She's Yours

The Perfect Conversation: Win Any Girl with Words

The 9 Laws of Attractive Body Language for Men

Understanding Sexual Attraction: What Makes a Woman Want You

120 Body Language Signals that She Likes You

CONTENTS

The Forbidden

Nothing is more exciting, and at the same time nerve racking, than the forbidden. Accessing forbidden information, especially when much of that information pertains to yourself, is another feeling all together. It was that desire for the forbidden that lead to this book.

At the time I had no idea that this desire would shatter the way I viewed the world. I had no idea that a peak behind the curtains would reveal a secret life.

We have entered a time of smart phones, social media, and messaging. These days, women spend more time sending messages than they do communicating face-to-face. This has an interesting aftereffect: almost everything they say has a record. Without knowing it, they write a journal of their lives—a journal composed of messages.

By reading these messages you begin to see a picture of what they did yesterday and the day before. You know what they said and who they said it to. You begin to build a real picture of who they are.

The thing that makes all this even more fascinating is that they don't believe anyone is watching, and because they don't believe there is anyone to judge them, you can see when they lie, when they cheat, who they really care for and whom they only pretend to care for. When they think nobody is watching, the same person you have spoken to countless times becomes somebody else suddenly and entirely.

The Key Logger

Years ago I installed a key logger on my laptop. I was curious to know if a girl that I was dating was talking to other guys. With that key logger, I was able to record her passwords for all the messengers and social media networks she had used. I didn't find what I expected.

As my life continued I kept the key logger on my computer, and gained access into the private lives of whomever I was dating at the time. I began seeing patterns and I started to record of a lot of the information that I found. I was able to see what they told their friends about me, what their friends said about me, whom they were talking to, what they were saying, where they went, and who they went with.

Was it an invasion of privacy? Absolutely. Would I recommend anybody to do the same? Of course not. However, I learned some very important, life changing lessons.

The world is not black and white, and neither are people. In this book I will talk about twelve very different types of relationships that I had with twelve very different types of women. In each of these twelve relationships I was able to see what they didn't want me to see, to know what they didn't want me to know.

I will tell you who I thought they were and who they turned out to be. I will show you the patterns that all the women showed; the things I can deduce about the TRUE nature of women because I was able to see the face they didn't want to show the world.

I will show the wealth of unknown knowledge that I uncovered in detail. The shocking truths are there, but the most astounding thing you will read is how many I have uncovered.

I will tell you a little about myself. I don't have model looks, nor am I bad looking. I am approaching my late twenties and I have an average income. I have become very good with women over the past few years and I can usually land any girl I want. The reason I tell you all this is because it affects the types of women that I have dated and the types of relationships that I have had.

Every one of the 12 girls in the relationships that I am about to describe are at least in the top 20% in terms of attractiveness for their age, and age-wise they are at their prime. These are girls that can pretty easily land a high value guy and all of them have plenty of options. This is imperative to know, because it's possible that less attractive women will act differently.

Before making any judgments about this book, all I ask is that you read it until the end. Many things will become clear in the conclusion.

All names and hints to who these women are will be withheld. I will start in order with the first of twelve girls. I will call her Number One.

Number One – The Caring Girl

I had been dating her for a bit and was honestly ready for a relationship. I was ready for the intimacy that comes along with being with the right girl.

I met Number One in a grocery store. She had an especially pretty face and when I saw that, I made up an excuse to talk to her. I asked her for help finding some food.

I remember how bashful she looked when she attempted to answer me, obviously not accustomed to talking to strangers. She was small, shy, and acted so innocent. I gave her my number and she texted me almost immediately.

We hit it off very quickly. Within a week we were spending most of our time together.

A couple weeks into the relationship an accident happened. I cut my hand and was walking through the courtyard of the place I was staying, looking for a first aid kit because of the amount of blood that was gushing out. Half way through the courtyard I passed out.

I woke up in the arms of somebody, having no idea where I was or what was going on. The next thing I remember after that is waking up again in the hospital.

I had hit my head and had a severe concussion. Over the next day I slowly recovered my memories and called Number One. As soon as she heard she was on her way to the hospital.

I spent the next day few days in the hospital and so did she. She slept in my bed with me and spent all day next to me. Bringing me food and running errands for me.

Those moments in the hospital, with my arm around her in the hospital bed as we slept, were the moments when my feelings for Number One started getting very strong. I got checked out of the hospital and we returned to day-to-day life.

I trusted Number One completely, but I had just learned about the key logger. The desire to know how honest she had been with me was too strong. I installed the key logger.

When she came over, she checked her Facebook and Yahoo Messenger and I was able to get her passwords. I checked her Facebook and she seemed to be a hundred percent faithful to me. I read some of her messages where she told friends about me. She told them how lucky she was and how she hoped for something more with me.

Then I checked her Yahoo messenger and noticed a conversation with a guy. The guy was currently out of town, but was going to return in a few weeks and wanted to meet her. It was during the time that I was going to be out of town. They had already agreed to meet the day he got back into town.

I was crushed. The moment I saw her again I asked her if I could trust her.

"Yes," she replied.

"Then open your Facebook for me."

As I already knew, there was nothing bad on there.

"Now open your Yahoo," I demanded.

She was hesitant then, making up an excuse so she wouldn't have to open it. I told her to open it and told her there was no future for us if she didn't. She opened it and I opened the messages with the guy that was out of town. I read them out loud and asked her to explain.

At first she tried lying, telling me that she wanted to meet him just as friends, but I pointed to a particular passage to prove that wasn't the case.

She spent the next twenty minutes trying to convince me how they were only friends. The messages made that scenario unlikely, and finally she said, "You will be gone for two months, I'm not sure if you will return, or if you will be faithful."

I had had enough. I told her to leave, and she cried and told me how she had made a mistake. I nearly had to force her out the door.

I spent the next few days reflecting on our relationship, sick to my stomach that she could do that to me. I reflected on all that she had done for me, our time in the hospital, and then how she had betrayed me.

We had not been an official couple, but it didn't feel like it was needed. It seemed so clear to me that we were in a relationship, even if we hadn't defined it. I was bombarded with article sized messages from her.

They started out saying how she did nothing wrong because we had not defined the relationship. I kept my silence, and her messages turned into expressions of love and regret.

These continued for days before I finally gave in and agreed to see her. I was very attracted to her and I felt like we almost picked up where we left off, but what she had done was always in the back of my mind.

A couple weeks passed and it was time for me to leave for two months. Our relationship had taken a step back, but she promised to be faithful to me and to be waiting when I returned. I made no commitment to her, because of what had happened.

She still had no idea that I had her passwords and I checked in on her from time to time.

One day, late at night, I was bored and decided to check her Yahoo. I saw a conversation with a guy and checked it out. It had been continued from somewhere else, possibly from text.

I read through it and that sick feeling in my stomach returned.

"Of course I like you."

"I can't wait to see you again," the stranger wrote.

As I read down I realized that this conversation was going on as I was reading. They had started to webcam, the conversation continued.

"Take it off." The guy said.

"Like this?" She replied.

"Yeah just like that."

The conversation got more and more explicit until I couldn't continue reading. I was reading what was happening as it was actually going on and I felt that sick feeling in my stomach, but worse than ever. I logged out and made a futile attempt to sleep.

The following weeks I received many messages from her.

"I miss you so much."

"I can't wait to see you again."

"I miss your kisses."

I rarely replied and ignored her when she asked me what was wrong. Eventually I stopped replying at all and when I returned to her city, I never told her I was there.

She would write countless love letters, thinking that the reason I would not respond was what had happened before. I wouldn't respond and the relationship slowly died away.

To this day I still get messages from her from time to time.

Number One Profile – The Caring Girl

Attractiveness: Very attractive girl. She could have her pick of men if she weren't so shy.

How I originally perceived her: Sweet, innocent and feminine. She had a young daughter, so I didn't see her as completely innocent, but as innocent as you could see a single mom.

How I perceived her after the key logger: From her messages it seemed that I was her first choice, but she could not go two months without other men. She constantly lied to me about her faithfulness. It was very difficult to get her to stop lying even as I showed her the messages.

Perceived Sluttiness: 2/10

Actual Sluttiness: 7/10

What I learned and how it affected me: I learned that women are very good liars. After installing the key logger, I never actually expected to find anything. I never doubted her faithfulness to me or how strongly she felt for me, but I learned the truth.

I learned that some women can't go long periods with a man. She cared deeply for me, maybe even loved me, but she still couldn't go without another man for two months.

I had been very trusting and I thought I could always see if a woman was lying to me. Maybe I still could, but I realized I couldn't one hundred percent fall into the fantasy of a perfect relationship after their declarations of love and descriptions of their feelings towards you. I became very suspicious, but I figured Number One must have been a chronic liar or something similar, and most women weren't like this. Right?

Number Two – The Motorcycle City Tour

I was just about to move to a new city and I didn't know anybody. I wanted to make some friends and start some possible relationships before I arrived.

I started meeting some girls online, before arriving I had been chatting with about seven girls that I found attractive. I kept contact with the seven girls and I was excited to meet all of them.

For my first night in the new city I set up a date with my favorite of the seven. Another short girl with an exotic looking face that was much more cute than sexy, even though she had all the right curves in all the right places.

My first night in the new city she arrived outside my hotel on her scooter. She said she was going to give me a tour of the city. She was even cuter in person and I hopped on the back of her scooter. We rode through the city, the cool night air blowing in my face as I wrapped my arms around her. This was the first moment I remember strong feelings developing for Number Two.

As the night went on we stopped in different spots and talked. Our personalities clicked. We were constantly laughing and enjoying each other's company and at the end of the night she dropped me off back at my hotel.

I told her I wanted to see her the next afternoon. At first she resisted, saying we should see each other the following day, but then she gave in.

The next day I awoke to a knock on my door. It was Number Two. She wanted to show me more of the city. I got dressed and we left.

We did another city tour on her scooter. It made me really understand why people love motorcycles. You are so shielded from the world when you are in a car, but on a motorcycle it feels like you are really there.

We spent the entire day together. Our time together feeling almost magical; the day was over before we knew what happened. She returned with me to my room that night and we spent the entire night together.

For the next week we spent nearly every moment together. We were both on short vacations from our jobs and there was only one place we wanted to be, together. We went on trips to other cities together and more trips on her scooter around the city.

During this time the six other girls I had promised to see barely entered my mind.

A day finally came when she had an obligation she had to attend to, so I had some time alone. I checked my key logger and logged into her Facebook.

She was talking with a few guys quite regularly. In fact, I looked and I saw that she had planned a date for the day after she met me. That was the reason that she had originally wanted to see me two days after our first night together. She had blown him off, but after the connection that I had felt it still kind of stung that she had tried to see him.

Then there was another guy that had invited her out to a club on the previous Friday night and she had agreed to see him. I thought back to the previous Friday night and I remembered her trying telling me she wouldn't be able to meet me.

"That's ok," I had replied.

"What will you do?" She asked me.

"If you are busy, then I guess I will go check out one of the clubs."

"Oh." And I saw a look of worry on her face. I think the fact that I would go without her made her jealous. "Well, maybe we could go."

"I thought you were busy?" I replied.

"I can probably cancel it."

Then as I looked at the messages, she cancelled her date with him.

It felt like another betrayal as we had spent nearly all of our time together for the previous three or four days. I started to get the familiar sick feeling in my gut as I continued reading.

She was getting messages from many guys trying to meet her. It was clear, women as pretty as her get a LOT of attention from guys on the Internet. She was even getting constant messages from one of her professors wanting to meet up.

I read some of the messages with guys a few weeks back. It looked like she had met a guy at a bar and then went to a club with him. It wasn't completely clear but I think they slept together.

She had been messaging him trying to see him again and he had been blowing her off, it looked like he had only been interested in sex. I looked at his profile, and he was a particularly good looking guy. She still kept contact with him.

I continued reading her messages and it became clear that she WAS really searching for a relationship.

The next time I saw her, I asked her a few questions. I asked her if she was talking to any other guys.

"No, just you," she replied.

"No other guys at all?"

"Well yeah… but just friends."

"Not anybody that is interested in you or anybody that you are interest in?" I asked.

"Of course not."

I tried to hide the sting of that lie. I continued asking her questions.

"When was the last time you had sex?" I asked.

"About three months ago. You?"

Another probable lie. All things pointed to her being pumped and dumped by the handsome guy from her Facebook a few weeks prior.

I answered her question, then asked, "How many guys have you been with?"

As she counted backwards with names and how long ago it was. It was three and they were all boyfriends. She still lied about being with the handsome guy a few weeks prior.

Again, my image of her was shattered. I asked to read her Facebook. Saying no at first, she finally agreed after I made it clear that for this relationship to continue she must show me.

She did, and I confronted her on her lies to me; the messages to the other guy, and how she had wanted to meet that other guy on Friday night.

Her replies to the past questions about sex were that she didn't want to remember.

Her reply to the question about seeing the other guy on Friday night was that she didn't end up doing it, that she ended up seeing me.

It didn't feel like it was enough and I told her that.

"I care about you so much," she started pleading.

She continued pleading and telling me about her strong feelings for me. She said that she hadn't felt as strong last Friday, but that now she was sure of her feelings. She wanted to be with me.

I was angry and sad for the next few days. I kept seeing her, but the rift had started. We continued spending time together and it seemed like she had forgotten her lies to me, wholeheartedly expressing her desire for a serious relationship.

However, I could not forget what happened and although I felt very strong feelings toward her, I was hesitant.

A week later I found out I would be leaving for two weeks. We spent the next week together and I didn't tell her I was leaving until I was getting in the taxi to the airport.

I broke the news to her there in front of the taxi with all my luggage.

She was shocked and angry. "You should have told me!" She screamed. I should have. She said she wasn't sure if she wanted to see me when I got back.

"You're right Number Two, I should have told you. I feel bad, but I will be back."

When I arrived at my destination I had many messages from her telling me she didn't mean it and that she was excited for me to return.

While I was gone I checked her Facebook and saw that she continued talking to the guys that had been trying to see her, even though she told me she wouldn't.

I slept with another girl and the next time I talked to her I asked her if she had been talking to other guys. She lied to me, of course. Then I told her I had been with another girl.

"Why are you doing this? You are tearing my heart out."

"At least I'm being honest about it." I replied.

A week later she started sending me messages that she couldn't wait for me to be back and that it was okay that I was with another girl because we weren't official when I left.

I saw on her Facebook that she met another guy while I was gone. I don't know what happened, and at that point I didn't care. I ignored her future messages and never saw her again.

To this day I still get random messages from her wanting to see me again, just like Number One.

Number Two Profile – The Motorcycle City Tour

Attractiveness: She was very cute and had a body with nice curves. She had a very unique face and her own type of beauty.

How I originally perceived her: Thanks to her cute looks, she was another girl that I saw as very innocent. She was older than Number One by about four years and I noticed it in maturity.

How I perceived her after the key logger: I saw she wasn't as innocent as I originally thought. Again, when I checked her Facebook I honestly didn't expect to find anything. However, because it seemed that she was searching for a relationship, I did feel like it was possible that if I 100% committed to her that she would have been faithful, but too many things had happened for that to be possible.

Perceived Sluttiness: 2/10

Actual Sluttiness: 4/10

What I learned and how it affected me: Attractive girls online most likely have a LOT of men chasing after them and Number Two was no exception. When a girl has a lot of options it's very easy for her to use them if things get a little rough.

I learned that just because I am spending the majority of my time with somebody, it doesn't mean I can assume she will stay a hundred percent loyal.

The thing that affected me the most was when she had planned to meet that guy on that Friday night and see me another day. It made me realize even though a girl is clearly into you in that moment when you are with her, it doesn't mean things can't change. I realized no relationship was set in stone and I became even more un-trusting with women.

Number Three - Selfless

I met her in the subway. We ended up standing near each other while the subway was pretty empty because of the late hour. I can't remember exactly what I said to her, but I remember how warmly she responded and from right off the bat she wanted to keep the conversation going. It felt so comfortable right from the start with Number Three. Comfortable is how everything felt as this relationship advanced.

Number three had a cute face and an even cuter personality. She was a traditional type girl. She was seven years older than me, but she looked to be the same age. She was in great shape, she had a curvy body, but not in any way chubby. She had boobs and ass and what seemed like the whole package. I am rarely attracted to anybody older than me, so it was a strange feeling. Even with her looks, it was her sweet personality that really won me over.

Things escalated fast with Number Three, although thanks to my now suspicious personality, I didn't let myself feel too much too quickly.

Number Three had gotten out of a seven year long relationship about a year prior to meeting me. It was clear that he had been her world; we would be talking and the next thing you know she would be going on about her ex-boyfriend. She told me how he had cheated on her, and then got the other girl pregnant and left Number Three for the other girl. She told me how he would call her and ask her to return to him and some nights she would. Doing exactly to the other girl what the other girl had done to her.

It bothered me that she talked about him, but I didn't let it get to my head. It was actually kind of charming how she had made him the center of her universe and I could understand how it would be hard to find something to talk about that didn't include the man you spent the last decade with.

The relationship continued and I started to get the "center of her universe treatment". Number Three absolutely loved doing things for me. Anything she could do to make my life a bit easier, she would. She wouldn't do it to try to impress me, but she would do it because it made her happy. I had never met a girl so selfless and with a desire this strong to do things for other people.

We had spent another day together during a local festival and we took a riverboat cruise. It was an amazing night that I will never forget and it further strengthened my feelings for her. After that night I started thinking if it was time to try for something more serious with Number Three; however, things never seem to be work out so easily.

One day as we were on a date, she answered a phone call. It was her ex. I got annoyed and said, "It's not ok to talk to him while you are with me."

We continued fighting about it and eventually I told her that I had been with other girls since I met her. She looked crushed. I felt guilty, but I mentioned how it felt like she was still in a relationship with her ex and I wasn't ready to commit.

She stormed out and would not reply to my messages for a couple days. I took a trip out of town for a few weeks. A few days later she answered me and said that she forgives me and she understands. She wanted to be with me and really give it a try. She said she would let go of her boyfriend and I could commit to her.

I accepted her offer to give it another try.

"I'm out of town and I won't be back for a couple weeks."

"But my birthday is in a week," she replied.

"I'm sorry."

She was crushed that I wouldn't be there for my birthday, but she only complained about it the once.

I continued my out of town trip and her birthday came and went. I got around to checking her Facebook and noticed some messages with a guy. They were playful, flirty, and mentioned that they had met. Then I checked a photo that she had uploaded. It showed that she had hid it from me. I looked at the photo.

It showed her and the guy sitting down next to each other in a bar. They were very close to each other and his hand was on her upper thigh. I felt that sick feeling in my stomach again.

She continued talking to me, acting as if nothing had happened. Deep confessions of her feelings for me were waiting whenever I checked my account. She couldn't wait for me to return. I responded, but I stayed cold and distant.

I asked her if she had met any other guys or had been talking to any other guys.

"Of course not." She would reply. She lied to me.

I told her I wasn't sure if I'd be able to make it back for a bit longer. She was pretty successful and had quite a bit more money than me. That is relevant because she really wanted to see me and offered to pay for my flight and to take care of me if I came right away.

I did want to see her. I accepted and was on a flight the next day. She was waiting for me when I arrived and I pretended like nothing had happened. It was so nice being with her, I didn't want it to end.

I remember sitting in my room, then hearing a knock on the door. She came in with foods from two different restaurants and a bunch of snacks from a gas station.

"I wasn't sure what you wanted to eat, so I bought many options," she said with a smile.

Later than night we watched a movie on my bed. I was eating sunflower seeds and she started breaking them in her mouth for me and then feeding them to me. She spent the rest of the movie breaking and feeding me the sunflower seeds as my eyes were glued to an action packed movie.

It still astounded me how much she enjoyed doing things for me. She wanted nothing other than to be by my side. That night I wasn't able to confront her about the photos. She had so many amazing qualities, how could I tell her goodbye.

The photos were eating away at me and the next time I saw her I had her open up her Facebook and I confronted her about the photos.

She responded with things like:

"It was my birthday and you were gone."

"You had been with other girls and I was sad."

"He kissed me and tried to come home with me, but I didn't let him. Even though I was drunk and it was my birthday I wouldn't do it. I care about you."

There was no way of knowing. I was with other girls while I was with her, so I couldn't be mad at her for kissing a guy, but I couldn't enter a relationship with a girl that had been with another guy after meeting me. But how could I know?

Her tear filled replies were enough to partially convince me. We continued dating. She took me on trips where that still feel like dreams. We rarely fought during that period and I can't think of anything other than warm, happy memories with her from then.

Eventually, the constant thought that she had slept with that guy made it's way from the back of my mind to my daily thoughts. She rarely mentioned her ex now, but when she did it made me wonder if she had returned to him as she had before. My doubts continued.

The relationship had been poisoned and even though she pampered me and was so sweet, it became too much. I told her goodbye.

"I can't do this anymore; I just don't feel like there is enough trust here. Maybe, in two years, we can try this again."

I continued to get messages from her, counting down until the two year mark. However, about six months ago they stopped. I really do hope she found the right guy.

Number Three Profile - Selfless

Attractiveness: She was very cute, however, maybe a few years past her prime. It was clear that in her youth she had guys falling all over her and killing themselves just to get a shot at a date with her. Still, she was quite attractive with a decent number of options.

How I originally perceived her: I have a weakness for a sweet and feminine personality and she had it. Her boyfriend of seven years showed she was definitely not the promiscuous type and I knew that being in a relationship was part of how she defined herself.

How I perceived her after the key logger: I still saw her as a sweet girl, but a sweet girl that will take an opportunity with another guy and lie about. I used to never believe that girls like her were capable of lying, I saw the world like a Disney movie; I was so blind.

Perceived Sluttiness: 2/10

Actual Sluttiness: 3/10

What I learned and how it affected me: Again I learned that a girl with options will use them if things aren't going well. Even though she was loyal to a fault at times, it didn't mean she wouldn't go for other guys. However, I really couldn't fault her for it because of what I had done to her. I still saw her as a good person, but I had seen too much and the lies slowly tore apart my feelings for her.

It was the fact that I didn't KNOW the truth. The doubts crept into my mind and my previous experiences had taught me to expect the worst. If she had never lied to me, I would have been able to completely trust her word... but she did lied to me and even afterwards continued to lie.

Number Four – Paris Hilton

I met Number Four late at night in a night club. Sometimes, there are girls that just dig your look and body language. I could see her attraction for me the moment we locked eyes. She actually came and talked to me, something that very rarely happens.

She had a cute face and a slender body. Overall, she was slightly less attractive than the previous three girls, but still attractive.

It became clear as I talked to her that she was quite wild. She had an extraverted and possibly party girl personality. It appeared she came from a family with money; she reminded me of Paris Hilton in so many ways.

After dancing with her, things escalated quickly and she ended up coming home with me that night. It was honestly a great night and the next day she expressed interest in spending New Years with me.

A friend and I were thinking about planning a trip to a nearby tourist city for New Years. It would be packed for the big day, but that would only make it better. We started making plans and I wondered if I would take her.

The next day I met another girl and we hit it off. She was a bit prettier than Number Four with a more sweet and feminine personality. After the new girl spent the night with me, I met up with my friend to finalize plans.

We were going. I called the girl from the night before, but she wouldn't pick up. I left some messages for her, but as the minutes passed by, she didn't reply.

We had waited until the last minute and we needed to leave that day. I thought back to Number Four and called her.

"Do you want to come?" I asked.

"I will be there in three hours," she replied.

My friend brought his girl and I brought number four and we were on our way to the start of a New Years adventure. While we were driving there I received a message from the girl from the night before:

"Sure, I would love to go."

Of course she responded: "Actually, we have already left."

"Well, I can meet you there," she responded.

"We can see each other when I get back."

I wanted to spend New Years Eve with her, but here I was with Number Four sitting next to me and there was no turning back now.

The four of us had a great time those first two days. Number Four really started growing on me. She was so passionate and that is the best way to describe our relationship… passionate.

Then, I got Number Four's password on my key logger and when I got some time alone I checked it.

As I read through her messages it was clear she was in contact with A LOT of guys. In fact, she had told a guy that was in our current city that she would be here and that they would meet up.

I was furious. I could understand that she had other guys and that was fine, because I had other girls. But to plan a meeting when she came there with me? The next moment I saw her I took her phone and checked it, showing her the messages.

She started out angry at me for looking at her messages.

"Sure it's all my fault. Get out." I motioned to the door of the hotel room.

She then changed her tone and started pleading, telling me that she wasn't actually going to meet him and that she just said she would because he is constantly asking to see her.

I continued my stance. I didn't want to be with her, and there was still time before New Years Eve to find a girl to kiss. "You should go," I told her.

She continued pleading with me, but I didn't budge. Then she got angry and started getting slightly violent with me. Suddenly, she did something I hadn't expected. She jumped into my arms and starting making out with me. The switch from anger to passion was so sudden that I hadn't expected it.

I felt the passion to and as she started grinding against me I threw her on the bed and had some of the best sex I had ever experienced.

I forgave her and we continued the trip together. New Years Day came and the four of us started drinking and planning out our night. It was a great day and we gathered in a famous street with tens of thousands of other people for the countdown.

The anger and charged passion was still there from the night before, but at the same time, the energy and excitement of the people around us was contagious. I didn't know what I felt towards her, it was just an unreadable blur of emotions.

5, 4, 3, 2, 1. Midnight arrived and our passion erupted as our lips met. My friend's girl took a photo of the two of us kissing. It looked like something out of a movie. The way the lighting hit the two of us, the obvious passion, and the crowd parting around us.

"I love you," she told me afterwards. For the rest of the night she would tell it to me every half an hour. Caught up in the moment, I almost said it back to her, but those are words I have rarely spoken to anyone, let alone a girl I had just met five days earlier.

We spent the next night drinking and living in the moment. At the end of the night, when we were returning to our hotel, I remember being half drunk and reflecting on the night and thinking, *this is by far the best New Years Eve I have ever had.*

I woke up the next morning next to Number Four. I felt a pain on my back and went to the mirror to see five scratch marks from her fingers from the night before and hickeys all over my body.

I went back to the bed. She was fast asleep. I looked at her phone lying on the bed next to her and my mistrustful behavior got the best of me. I grabbed it and looked through it as she slept.

A month or so earlier she had broken up with her ex-boyfriend. He was a doctor and he had left her for another girl. I saw a message from him from two hours earlier.

The message read: "I miss you."

"I miss you too," she had replied.

"I think I still love you."

"Me too."

After the night we just had, she had responded to him like this… I woke her up and showed her the messages.

"I didn't mean it. I was half asleep. I love you! I don't love him anymore."

I felt more anger than I had felt in a long time and told her to get out. I started packing her things into her suitcase as she continued pleading.

I packed her suitcase and motioned towards the door. Again, her pleading turned into anger as she started screaming at me.

"I know you have other girls too!" She screamed. Then the insults came and I started getting angry.

"Get out," I said, barely able to control my voice.

She refused and I took her suitcase and put it outside the door. Then I returned for her. I picked her up and literally carried her to the door. She kicked and screamed then clung to the archway with her hands so I couldn't pull her through. I finally got her through the door, put her down, and tried to shut it. She pushed her foot into the door and started pleading again. I was having trouble getting the door shut without hurting her.

"Please forgive me, I didn't mean what I said. Just let me in and we can talk about it calmly."

I finally gave in and let her in on the condition that she left in five minutes. She immediately came to me and tried kissing me, grinding up next to me and taking off articles of clothing.

I stopped her from removing any more and five minutes later I told her to leave. She continued pleading, but now she was calmer. She finally agreed to go.

"Ok, but if I go, then we are done forever."

"Ok," I replied.

She left and I closed and locked the door.

Thirty seconds later I hear the door trying to be opened, then pounding on the door. Her pleading continued, but I tuned it out and ignored it. I stayed in my room for four hours until my friend came up and told me she had left.

She randomly showed up at the hotel the next couple of days. I ignored her and told that it was over between us.

A week later, back in the town we met, I got a message from her saying that she was outside of my place. She said that she only wanted to talk, as friends. She called me and she seemed calm over the phone so I went outside and met her.

She looked smoking hot. She was dressed to the nines, in a tight black dress that really showed her curves. My old feelings of passion surfaced moments after seeing her.

The next thing I knew she was pleading with me again, saying she loved me and wanted to be with me.

"If we are official, I won't talk to any other guys. I promise. I love you," she said.

Feeling tons of desire welling up I finally gave in.

"Ok," I said, "But you have to let me see your phone so I know that you are serious."

"Fine," she replied and handed me her phone.

"I started going through her messages and she calmly watched, then as I opened her Skype she asked for her phone back. She started getting mad and I kept the phone just out of her reach as I read the messages.

I opened her most recent messages. They were from about an hour earlier. She had set up a meeting with another guy and had went to see him. Then they had started fighting when he had wanted her to go straight to his room. She had refused and he had told her to fuck off.

She had gone from where she was supposed to meet him, straight to my place. Wow, what was wrong with this girl? I gave her the phone back.

"Goodbye Number Four."

She started pleading as I walked away. Grabbing my arm and trying to get me to talk to her. She was crying and screaming and making a scene.

She wouldn't let me go back to my place without taking her along as well. She clung to my side. I looked at her again, finally seeing her for who she was. I was still angry.

"Come with me," I lead her back to my place.

I didn't respond to her at all. When we got to my room I threw her on the bed, pulled off her dress and literally tore off the remainder of her clothes.

It was angry and passionate and amazing.

I said goodbye to her the following morning, giving vague answers about our future.

The following weeks I continued getting messages from her, but I never responded again.

Number Four Profile – Paris Hilton

Attractiveness: She had a decent face and a good body. She had more options than any of the other previous girls by far, but that was due to her partying all the time and the sexy clothes she would wear.

How I originally perceived her: She was obviously a party girl, but she could also be charming. At times it seemed like she was really looking for a relationship.

How I perceived her after the key logger: It was clear she WAS looking for a relationship; however, this girl needed constant attention from men. She had many prospects and because she was very sexual, she would use them. She was somewhat bipolar and being around her you would feel bipolar as well. I would go from feeling like the two of us were on top of the world to hating her guts… within minutes.

Again the key logger changed how I saw this girl.

Perceived Sluttiness: 7/10

Actual Sluttiness: 9/10

What I learned and how it affected me: Treat a slutty girl like a slutty girl. Don't even entertain the idea of a relationship, no matter how amazing you feel when you are with her, because there will be other men.

I began to understand that it is the nature of women to be pursuing multiple men and I began to accept it. I stopped looking for relationships; it was pretty painful to have felt so much for this girl, then to learn that she lied to me. Maybe I was meant for less serious relationships.

Number Five – The Rich Girl

I was out late at night partying with some friends and as I was walking through the club I locked eyes with a cute Asian girl. She had a beautiful face and I continued walking a few steps, stopped, turned around and introduced myself to her. She didn't open up to me at all at first and the music was so loud it was difficult to communicate.

I took out my phone and we started communicating by writing messages in notepad. I flirted with her through our messages as I started into her eyes. It came off as pretty charming.

Her face was clearly her best feature, all centered around these absolutely beautiful eyes. She was short with a typical Asian body. I guessed she came from money because of her somewhat snobby attitude, even though she did seem slightly interested in me, and her designer clothing.

Next thing I knew it was 6 am and the club was closing. The bouncers started ushering people out and she told me she would meet me outside. I started looking for my friends, calling and texting them, but they were nowhere to be found. I waited outside the club, and continued waiting…

She gave me the slip. I had been waiting for over twenty minutes, she must already be gone.

I was about to leave when somebody tapped me on the shoulder. It was Number Five. I had thought for sure she had already left.

She told me she knew of a bar that was still open and she led me down the street towards the new bar.

She was difficult to read and I was having trouble telling how into me she was. I decided to find out. I grabbed her hand and pulled her to face me. Then I quickly pulled her to me by her hips and kissed her.

She was surprised, but accepted the kiss, and then gave more back. She started getting more passionate with the kiss and I pulled away; it's best to leave her wanting more.

We got some more drinks at the bar she had mentioned and stayed there for a while, continuing our conversation via notepad on my cell phone. Then I started noticing it getting light outside. It was 8 am.

"I'm tired, let's go sleep," I told her.

"Where at?"

"My place isn't too far."

"I don't think so," she said with a smile. "Let's keep the night alive."

"Ok." I agreed, not ready to give up.

She knew of a private beach on the other side of the city that she said was amazing. When we got there we took off our shoes and walked along the beach together. We would stop every hundred meters or so to have a quick make session. After an hour of walking on the beach we got hungry and went to a little beach side seafood place. After eating a tasty sea food meal she called somebody to come pick her up.

"We will drop you off, and then I will have him take me home," she told me.

"Who is coming?" I asked.

"My driver."

Yeah, she was a rich girl. He picked us up and brought us to my place. She got out with me and told her drive that she would call him.

"I thought you were going back to your place?" I asked. She just smiled back.

We walked into my place and it was clear that she started getting uncomfortable. I wasn't living in the fanciest place and she definitely noticed.

"You are staying here?" She asked me with a look of disgust. She continued mentioning things she found disgusting and I tried to think of how I could turn this around.

"Oh, I'm sorry Princess, are these sheets only 600 thread count? My two million thread count sheets are being cleaned."

I started grilling her about being high maintenance until she started telling me that she wasn't and stopped complaining all together. My teasing had worked and she was getting comfortable.

We laid together and she really didn't seem like she wanted to have sex. We went to bed and the next day we woke up and I tried again. This time she was more open to it, but as I tried it was excruciatingly painful for her. I tried for the next couple of hours and not knowing why it would hurt her so bad I finally asked her:

"Are you a virgin?"

She just shrugged and we continued. It didn't make any sense that I would meet a virgin in a club, but I couldn't see any other reason why it would hurt her to this extent. An hour later, after the same problem, I asked her again.

"Are you a virgin?"

"Yeah," she replied.

Now it made sense. I was finally able to make it work and we spent every moment of the next few days together. Eating together, sleeping together, and simply enjoying each other's company. She threw money around like I had never seen.

After promising to see her again, I left and attended to my obligations. While I was away I checked my key logger for her Facebook password and read through her messages. She had her share of orbiters, but it was pretty clear she had friend zoned them. There was only one guy she constantly messaged.

It turns out she was in a relationship and he had been out of town on some business deals. I read further and he mentioned a medical issue.

It turns out he had done something during sex that had hurt her and that she had went to the doctor to try to repair the damage. Something down there had torn and that was why it was so painful for her to have sex.

She had lied to me about being a virgin and had never mentioned having a boyfriend. Reading through her messages it was pretty clear it was a pretty serious relationship with marriage close in the future.

After reading that I blew her off for the next week and finally I said, *screw it*, and called her. She answered and was angry that I hadn't been returning her calls. She said she didn't want anything like that and told me it was over. I told her ok and I haven't talked to her since.

Number Five Profile - The Rich Girl

Attractiveness: She had a very pretty face and an alright body. She was pretty attractive, but seemed even prettier because she took care of herself and wore expensive clothing.

How I originally perceived her: I met her in a club and I will usually be wary of any girl I meet in a club for anything serious, but there was something different about her. She seemed sweet.

How I perceived her after the key logger: A girl who can cheat on her boyfriend, even after we had such a great time and clicked, is still not a girl I'm interested in having anything serious with.

Perceived Sluttiness: 4/10

Actual Sluttiness: 5/10

What I learned and how it affected me: Because she seemed pretty loyal, up until me, I learned that if a girl gives a guy any window, it's possible for him to take it. I started realizing that a girl's faithfulness many times has to do with the amount of game of the kinds of guys that chase her.

Number Six – Internet Stalker

Number Six I met online. I had been talking with her for a couple days, but I had recently met a girl I liked and wasn't that interesting in meeting her. She continuously messaged me, asking me when we could meet.

I blew her off for a while before responding, "I'm just at home watching a movie, but if you want to stop by for fifteen minutes, you can."

An hour later she was at my door knocking. Number Six was very young; she had just turned 18, and was more attractive in person than in her photos. I would have met her sooner had I known she was this cute.

She ended up staying much more than 15 minutes as we talked and flirted. Things escalated quickly and since we were watching the movie on my bed. One thing led to another and we slept together. I hadn't used my key logger in a while so I asked to see some of her pictures on Facebook, the ones she wouldn't let anybody see.

She showed me some sexy photos that she had set so only she could see them. She had plenty, not necessarily a good girl, even though she was so young. It was getting late and she had to be home soon so we called it a night.

After she left I checked her Facebook. She had over three thousand friends and more orbiters than I could count. She had to have been consistently messaging over fifty guys with hopes at something more with her.

She called wanting to see me again, and I continuously blew her off. A week or so later I checked her Facebook and noticed some messages. She had looked at all my friends, most of them were girls, and she had messaged them saying to stay away from me.

She had messaged one of the girls I had liked. I noticed soon after the messages that she had gone cold and not wanted to see me. Number Six had told her how we had sex and that now we were dating. Wow.

I started messaging the girl I like, trying to explain, but she wasn't interested and I never saw her again. Thanks Number Six.

I was practicing with a local University basketball team for exercise and one of the guys came up and mentioned her, saying, "I didn't know you were dating Number Six."

I thought that her 3000 friends on Facebook was her just wanting to add everybody, but maybe she did have a ridiculously large social circle.

"Not dating her," I replied.

I cut my losses and started completely ignoring Number Six.

I still get random messages from her from time to time.

Number Six Profile – Internet Stalker

Attractiveness: She had a cute face and an average body, but I'd say the previous five girls I have mentioned were cuter.

How I originally perceived her: I knew she wasn't a perfect girl because she was willing to come straight to my place, although I didn't think I would have been so attracted to her. I just thought she was a young girl with a crush.

How I perceived her after the key logger: I saw her as a deceptive girl, maybe even slutty as she had a small army of orbiters. I saw her as a girl that needs huge amounts validation and has no problem creating any drama.

Perceived Sluttiness: 5/10

Actual Sluttiness: 6/10

What I learned and how it affected me: I saw more of the deceptive nature of women and how many will do whatever it takes to get what they want. They will ruin your relationship with any girl if they think it will help them to land you.

After Number Six, I was more careful in the future with casual flings being able to contact other girls.

Number Seven – The Cuckold

I met Number Seven online as well. Set up a meeting with her at a restaurant right next to where I was staying. It wasn't too much work setting up getting her to go out with me.

She arrived and I noticed she had a bit of an awkward personality. She was introverted, but it seemed clear she was very sexual as well. Her face wasn't that pretty, but she had an amazing body.

Our conversation didn't feel that natural, it felt like work to me since she was so introverted. Our personalities didn't click, but I was very attracted to her. I went for it anyways and a few hours after meeting her we were back in my room.

I was right, she had an amazing body. I was very attracted to this girl, even though I'm pretty sure I was thinking with the wrong head.

We spent the entire night together, with sexy photo shoots and games. It was a pretty good time, but I remember after getting ready for another go at sex that she said something very odd.

"You don't have to wear a condom and you can cum inside of me. If I get pregnant you will never have to worry about paying child's support or hearing from me again."

I thought about it, but turned down the offer. She seemed pretty slutty and I didn't want to risk any diseases. Also, the idea of what she was proposing seemed crazy to me.

After she left the next day, I checked my key logger. I was able to get the password of her email. I looked through it and I noticed constant messages to a guy. They were filled with all types of nude photos of her and promises of marriage.

Then I read more. The guy was sending her money, a lot. They were dating and I remember him telling her in one of the messages, "I'll start sending you more when you are pregnant. You'll have to be eating for two."

These two were trying to have a baby. It looked like they had only been trying for a couple weeks, and this girl was trying to get me to knock her up. Poor guy.

Number Seven Profile – The Cuckold

Attractiveness: I'd say she was completely average in attractiveness; however, she changes from average to pretty hot once you see her body.

How I originally perceived her: I knew she was slutty just by seeing her body language. I could tell she liked male attention and, with the body she had, she would get it. She would accentuate her curves with tight dresses and give a little taste with revealing clothing.

How I perceived her after the key logger: I knew she was slutty when I met her and from how easily I was able to hook up with her, what I didn't expect is that she would so easily screw over a guy so she could have my baby.

Perceived Sluttiness: 8/10

Actual Sluttiness: 8/10

What I learned and how it affected me: The genetics of a girl's baby is much more important than any girl wants us to know. The only way women can continue choosing the father and having a guy that is more obtainable raise the child, is to let men know of how common it is. My only regret is not calling the guy before she changed her password.

Number Eight – Brother Boyfriends

I met Number Eight one night out at a club with some friends. We were sitting down at a table and her group of friends came over and started talking to us. It was clear right away that I was very attracted to Number Eight.

She had this young, good girl look; a cute face with a shy smile and a submissive, giggly personality. Even with this look, you could still see that she wasn't a good girl. It was a strange thing to see. Years earlier, judged on appearance alone, I would have one hundred percent believed she was the perfect girl to bring home to mom.

I continued talking to her and it seemed like we clicked. I could see she was interested in me.
My friends and I were about to go to a new place, so I got her number before we left. I enjoyed the rest of the night, but ended up texting her when I got home. I trusted my gut that she wasn't the good girl that she tried to be perceived as and asked her to come over and hang out for a bit.
"Sure," she replied with no convincing.
Good thing I had gotten better at reading these things. She showed up at my door, and this clearly sexual "good girl" came in she ended up spending the night with me, but some odd things she said stuck out.
By the end of the night, she was confessing some very strong feelings to me in an unnatural way. It was almost as if she was forcing it. I could tell she liked me, but her feelings didn't seem completely congruent with her words. On top of it all she was already hinting at a serious relationship with me.
The next day I got her Facebook password and checked some of her messages. It absolutely blew my mind.
This girl was telling about fifteen guys daily that she loved them. Most of those guys thought they were officially dating her.
On top of that, she would throw in little hints of certain gifts that she would love while talking to her many "boyfriends."

I had never seen anything like it. It was clear that this good girl act worked for her. She had many guys in love with her, giving her whatever she asked from them. No wonder this girl didn't work, she didn't have to.

After reading this I saw her a few more times. It kind of sickened me what she was doing, so I didn't feel bad toying with her. Hinting at a relationship and all the things I would buy her and places I would take her, but then telling her an obstacle between us that made it not possible. She would do whatever I wanted to try to convince me that we could overcome the obstacle lying in the way of us having a serious relationship.

I grew tired of it quickly and started ignoring her calls.

Number Eight Profile – Brother Boyfriends

Attractiveness: A pretty attractive girl with a very powerful "good girl" face.

How I originally perceived her: Her good girl face could not hide her nature. After all my experience I saw it, but I knew many less experienced guys could not see it so easily.

How I perceived her after the key logger: I expected she had a couple guys around, but never to the extent that I saw. She was pretty much running a boyfriend business and capitalizing on gifts.

Perceived Sluttiness: 8/10

Actual Sluttiness: 9/10

What I learned and how it affected me: I learned that it is important to understand what it is a girl wants from a relationship before you jump into it. This girl was using tons of guys that thought they were in a committed relationship with her. If they paid closer attention they would see the truth.

Number Nine – The Lies that Poison

I met Number Nine at a bus stop. She was obviously cute and I wasn't sure which bus route I was supposed to take. I asked her instead of the older guy next to her. I threw in the charm right from the get go, keeping the conversation very harmless but I was a hundred percent on with my body language.

She was hooked very quickly and I could see it. This girl was my type. She had it all: beautiful face, all the right curves and a cute personality. It actually happened that the bus she was taking was the one I wanted. We continued talking and it was clear everything was going perfectly.

After I saw that she didn't have much to do that day, I invited her to go grab something to eat with me. She accepted. We spent the rest of the day together. We ate together and went to movies. We talked all day long everything just absolutely clicked.

I remember sitting next to her while watching a movie. I usually don't like the first kiss with a girl to be at a movie theater for many reasons, but I literally couldn't stop myself from doing it. My desire to taste her lips was far stronger than my usual common sense.

It didn't matter; it felt like she had been waiting for the kiss as well and accepted it hungrily. The rest of the night we walked through downtown talking, only stopping to kiss.

It seemed so natural when I invited her back to my place. It already felt like I had known her for so long.

When we got to my room, I couldn't hold back from kissing her. I loved her lips and her smell. Everything just felt like it fell so perfectly into place.

She stayed the night with me and the following days we couldn't get enough of each other. She would go home only to change clothes and then she would return.

We were both on vacation and we would spend the days finding things to do around the city, then returning to my place and spending all our time kissing, talking and setting the sheets on fire. It seemed like we were always glued together, as close to each other as we could physically get.

During this time I asked her many questions. She told me about her boyfriend of many years that she had broken up with about six months earlier and how it had ended.

It was a while before I had enough time free from her to use the key logger. To be completely honest I had really strong feelings for this girl and having spent all that time with her I was sure she wouldn't lie to me; it wasn't part of her nature. She was so sweet and innocent it didn't seem physically possible.

I opened up her Facebook and looked at her messages. She wasn't talking with very many guys at all in a romantic way, but then I saw the messages with her ex-boyfriend. They were actually messages that were being sent at that moment.

I read as he would continually confess his love to her, begging her to take him back. He told her how he wanted to marry her and how he would spend all day thinking about her.

What bothered me was how she would reply.

"I love you too, but I can't continue, not after what you did."

They continued this and he begged to see her. She finally accepted. It twisted my stomach as this girl I had come to care about so much had agreed to meet her ex-boyfriend.

I texted her asking what she was doing. Of course she lied to me. There she was seeing a guy who was madly in love with her, hours after being with me.

It seemed so impossible that a girl this sweet could do this. She had also lied about who her ex-boyfriend was. She had shown me a picture of somebody different.

The next day she came over and I pretended not to know anything. Then when she opened her Facebook I asked to see and went straight to the messages with her ex-boyfriend.

She had told me she hadn't been with a guy for six months, but it was clear she had been with him about a month prior. She tried to shut it, but I told her to let me see or she would never see me again. She let me and I confronted her about seeing her boyfriend and what had happened. I also asked her why she lied about who it was.

She started crying and trying to explain herself, but the fact that she could so easily lie to me was a bitter pill to swallow. I felt so much for this girl in so little time that it terrified me.

I told her that it was best if we didn't see or speak to each other anymore. That it was best to stay away while our strong feelings for each other were forgotten. It was so difficult to kick her out as she stood there crying, but I couldn't accept the lies, not from her.

The next day she sent me a long message about how she only wanted to be my friend and she wanted to come help me look for an apartment. I missed her so much, so I told her that it was ok on the condition that it was only as friends.

Shortly after she arrived at my place it wasn't long before we were making out. I was an addict and she was my cocaine. The lies still ate away at me, but I couldn't tell this girl goodbye for lies like this. I understood that she had been with him for a long time, I tried to accept it.

We continued our relationship and it felt like things got more serious fast. She really wanted me to come to her home town and meet her family. I was hesitant, but in the end I couldn't resist. I had a desire to see her every hour of every day and I didn't want to spend time away from her when she went to visit her parents.

She somehow found out about that somebody saw her Facebook and changed her password, but not before I noticed the way she would still talk to her ex-boyfriend. It ate away at me. I told her that we could be together on the condition she would not talk to her ex-boyfriend. It was a mistake and my paranoia was obvious when I was with her.

I constantly accused her of talking to him. I had no real proof, but my gut was telling me that she was.

As I continued dating her the paranoia grew. One day as she was sleeping next to me, I reached for her phone. I started opening it when she awoke suddenly and got very defensive. She was hiding something. I was sure it was messages from him.

I felt locked in a cage; my feelings for her keeping me with her, but the lies keeping me unhappy.

One day when she had told me she was out of town I got a message from her and at the bottom of the message it displayed the location from where it was sent; it was her home town. The same town where her ex-boyfriend lived, but she had told me she was somewhere else.

I freaked out. I said some things in the moment and told her I never wanted to see her again, deleting every single way to contact her.

"Ok. If that's what you want that's fine, I'm not going to explain everything because of your insecurities." That was part of the message I received from her. She was right about one thing, seeing that she could lie to me did make me insecure about our relationship.

I continued complete silence for about a week, but I couldn't get her out of my head. After feeling pure emotional pain for days straight, I finally gave in and called her. She accepted my apology and said that we could see each other again, but with the condition of only being friends. Logically I knew I should just forget this girl, but something wouldn't let me.

When I saw her the next time she was very cold. We spent a while together with friends and it was torture seeing her act like this. When we were finally alone at the end of the night I confronted her, then she gave me some interesting news. She was ten days late on her period.

She had been lying to me, but it wasn't for the reason that I had expected. We reconciled and I told her I would buy what she needed to be sure.

It wasn't long before she found out she wasn't pregnant, but the relationship was poisoned.

For the first time I really started doubting if the key logger was a good thing overall. It had made me so paranoid about such an amazing connection. A few lies about things that really weren't that important had torn apart our connection from the inside out.

I continued to see Number Nine, but it was never the same. We would always end up kissing at the end of the night, but any possible future had been destroyed.

Number Nine Profile – The Lies that Poison

Attractiveness: A very attractive girl in almost every imaginable way. A good girl who only knew long-term relationships.

How I originally perceived her: I saw her as this sweet and innocent girl from a smaller town that had only had serious relationships with a loving and caring personality.

How I perceived her after the key logger: I saw that the long term relationship came with its baggage. I saw that even though she seemed so sweet and innocent she was still deceptive. I especially saw this as she strung along her ex-boyfriend as we were together, even accepting money from him.

Perceived Sluttiness: 1/10

Actual Sluttiness: 2/10

What I learned and how it affected me: Number Nine really got to me. For the first time I saw a girl lie, but I saw that they were possibly lies I was willing to live with. I saw how the key logger had torn apart our relationship. The fact that I had expected trust, without really building it, was something I had to learn from.

Number Ten – The Gay Friend Facebook Journal

I met Number Ten online. She was definitely one of the types of girls that get hundreds of messages a day so it was difficult to finally get her out on a date. When I finally met her I knew I had her twenty seconds after meeting her. I had flawless body language and after some good eye contact I could see clearly her attraction towards me.

Every once in a while you will find a girl that absolutely digs your look; this was one of those girls. The only way I can describe this girl is sexy. However, she had a shy, good girl persona that I didn't expect from talking to her online. The rest of the date was basically me not saying anything to mess up her clearly intense attraction for me. The date went very smoothly and she was back at my place before long. Everything was simply easy. I didn't feel like I had to try at all, it just happened.

I can honestly say I didn't love this girl's personality; it pushed me away from having any real feelings for her. However, sexually we just clicked. It made me want to continue seeing her and, as she was a sexual girl, I don't think she minded very much. When I first asked Number Ten how many guys she had slept with that first night she had replied, "Three." Seeing how sexual this girl was, I immediately called her out on it.

"Ok. Ok. Five."

I tried to call her out on it again, but she stayed there saying that's how many she had been with. I gave up and asked her another question.

"How long ago was the last time you have been with a guy?"

"About six months," she had replied.

When she went home I checked her Facebook and it seemed pretty clear that both those things had been lies. Maybe she had been with five guys in her life, but it didn't seem likely, and she had definitely had sex within a month.

I looked at her messages with guys. This girl had a lot of orbiters, and she would use them. They would take her on dates to various places and buy her gifts.

On top of that it looks like I had just entered a love triangle. There was a guy she really liked that she had been dating for a while that was starting to lose interest in her. We will call him Guy #1. Guy #1 was very artistic just like Number Ten. They had a long history that also included an abortion. They spent a lot of time together, but it seemed like he didn't want a serious relationship anymore.

The other guy in the triangle was a newer guy that she had met online. This dude looked like a male model; really handsome face and he really put in time on his body. He was the kind of guy that was always posting shirtless modeling photos on his Facebook, but it didn't look like he had much game.

I looked at her messages as she would tell Guy #1 and #2 how much she cared for them, minutes after leaving my room. They both asked her why she was busy the night she met me.

"Oh just out with some friends." She replied.

Then I found the gold mine; her gay best friend. She shared everything with him, although I would later learn that she even lied to him, even though it was only about small details. The conversations with him were basically her journal. I had entered the completely forbidden and it was full of shocking information.

We clicked sexually so I would see her about once or twice a week for the coming months. As our relationship progressed I would check in from time to time with her messages with her gay best friend.

It was clear after meeting me that she had completely lost interest in Guy #2, but she still held onto the guy she had dated before. She talked about her three guys saying that she has strong feelings for Guy #1 and I, but that for the model guy, who kept confessing his love to her, she feels nothing.

"Hahaha," she would write after telling this to her gay best friend.

I saw her a few more times and it looked like she was starting to not care about the other guy. She had made it clear that she wanted to be official with me, but how could I agree to that when she had so many guys she would tow around and another guy she had feelings for. However, things did start to change.

She started writing poetry for me about how strongly she felt about me. She told her gay best friend how, after being with me, she didn't know if it was possible to go back to normal guys. A night after seeing me she told her gay best friend about the guy she was obsessing over before meeting me:

"Now I look at photos of him and think 'Omg, what is that?' He just can't compare to having a guy like (my name)."

The next time I saw her she promised that she would be completely faithful to me, because she didn't want anybody else in her life. I didn't make the same commitment, but I told her that if it seemed like she was keeping that, maybe we could be more.

As you read earlier from her messages, she was not only slightly obsessed with me, but maybe even thought she was in love, which is exactly what makes what happens next so baffling.

One day I noticed that she went out on a Friday night with Guy #1. She had told me she was busy that day and when I read it I just felt anger. Anger that she could confess her love to me and promise to stay faithful, then, days later, to go spend a Friday night with the last guy she was in love with.

I wanted to confront her about it, so I called her. She didn't answer at first, but I got a call fifteen minutes later.

"Hey!"

"Hey, what are you up to?"

"Oh, just getting dinner with my sister, it's her birthday," she lied.

"Ah so you are in the car with her?"

"Yeah."

"Oh tell her happy birthday for me," I said.

She hesitated, not saying anything.

"Aren't you going to tell her?"

"He says happy birthday," I heard her mumble.

"I didn't hear her reply. Can I talk to her?"

"Now isn't a good time."

"You aren't with your sister are you?" I asked.

"I've got to go bye." Her voice was shaking and I could hear it through the phone. After that I sent her a message telling her not to call me anymore, that we are finished, and an hour later she showed up at my place crying.

She tried to stick with her story, telling me she was with her sister. When it was clear I didn't believe it, she told me she was with a friend, but with a guy that nothing would ever happen.

That was also clearly a lie, since he was the only other guy she had feelings for. She continued trying to lie for hours, not aware that I had a cheat sheet.

Finally she admitted that she used to date him and that yes, she had slept with him, but not for months. It was most likely still a lie, but I couldn't be sure.

Luckily, I didn't have very strong feelings for this girl, maybe partly because I could see how many guys she toyed with. I just accepted her for what we had, an amazing sexual connection and forgave her, but told her never to see or talk to him again. I didn't think she would do it, but it seemed like the right thing to ask.

Over the next weeks I continued checking her messages. With her messages with Guy #1, it seemed like she had told him that she was interested in me, and she was blaming him for me not wanting to be her girlfriend. He acted like he supported her pursuit of me, but he didn't exactly feel guilty for almost ruining our relationship, of course.

Number Ten continued writing about her feelings for me. She spoke to her gay best friend about our sexual connection:

"When I think about him, my legs tremble. I want him so bad."

It was still clear that she had strong feelings for me. However, I started to see a pattern. Whenever I wouldn't answer a call or I would postpone our relationship being official, she would run to another guy. She would ask him to take her out saying how much she missed him.

During one of these dates, one of her orbiters finally confessed his love to her after they both returned home:

"I have always loved you Number Ten, I haven't been able to say it, but I can't hide it anymore."

"I'm so sorry!!! I am dating somebody ☐." She went on to describe me. Poor orbiter. Poor guy should have done it in person. It's easier to have courage when you don't have to look the girl in the eye and women know this. If you look like a coward, women will lose attraction. On top of that if he told her in person, some guy with a key logger wouldn't be able to witness his sad story.

A day later a boyfriend from a year earlier confessed that he was still in love with her and that he would do anything to be with her again.

"I'm so sorry!!! I am dating somebody ☐." She gave him the exact same answer as the orbiter from the day before.

Even though this girl loved toying with men, it was clear that her feelings and attraction for me were real, although at times it was a little intense.

I saw some messages with her gay best friend when she was saying what would happen if I got her pregnant.

"Maybe he would finally commit," she said.

"Or maybe he would leave you," her gay best friend replied.

"I would just sleep with (Orbiter #1, Orbiter #2, Guy #1 or Guy#2) and tell them it was theirs. Then I could have (My Name's) beautiful baby and have a guy that would take care of me," she replied laughing.

"Well make sure to not wear a condom," her gay best friend joked back.

Even though there were some haha's in there, the conversation helped me see the true nature of women. This girl was half serious and it seemed like precautions for getting pregnant were the last things on her mind when she was with me. In fact, it seemed like she went out of her way not to take those precautions.

At other times she would talk about how she could end up with a husband like me and she would joke about using a love potion.

Her obsession with getting such a long term commitment started to bother me, especially since I wouldn't even agree to be her boyfriend.

I pushed it all aside in my mind. I had an incredible time when I was with this girl and I just had to accept her for what she was. She was unbelievably sexy, but I would never let her be my girlfriend, let alone my wife and it was all because of the tons of lies and deceptions.

I continued to see her once or twice a week, but I noticed she started acting more loyal, except for the fact that she spent a ton of time with guy #1. I accepted that maybe they were just friends and maybe I could at least give her a shot.

Then I logged into her online dating account. I saw the ridiculous amount of messages she received every day. She ignored about 98% of them, but she would reply every once in a while to the guys with the model type looks.

It made me realize that even though this girl was borderline obsessed with me, she wanted more options.

She saw that it bothered me and offered to erase her online profile.

"Ok," I replied.

She put off erasing it for a while then finally erased it. A day later I checked her email and she had opened up another dating profile on a different site. She hadn't even lasted 24 hours. Wow.

Maybe if I committed to her, she would stop looking and go all in for me, but I wasn't ever going to ever give her that opportunity, not after all the lies.

Number Ten Profile – The Gay Friend Facebook Journal

Attractiveness: Very attractive. Very sexy with curves that made every man in sight desires her.

How I originally perceived her: She had a shy good girl personality, but there was still an artistic liberal side that I could see. I knew that she was not the good girl that so many girls pretend to be off the bat.

How I perceived her after the key logger: I saw that, as usual, she was even more promiscuous than I had originally guessed. I was getting much better at reading women and seeing what is behind the persona they try to show the world, but still I was a bit surprised.

Perceived Sluttiness: 5/10

Actual Sluttiness: 7/10

What I learned and how it affected me: A woman's love of men telling her how pretty she is and how much they care about her is much more than any man would expect. What a man should expect is that he could be one of those guys that she uses to feel better about herself. She may lead a guy on that she is never interested in having something with, because it makes her feel good.

Number Ten's lies weren't that hard on me, partly because I expected them. One of the best ways to protect yourself against a woman is to know what she could do, no matter what type of good girl image she tries to show the world. To be honest Number Ten helped me accept the bad in women and get rid of quite a bit of my desire to completely own a girl.

Number Eleven - Acceptance and the Serious Relationship

Number Ten taught me so much. I saw a girl that was in love with me, and I saw how she would cushion my rejection by turning to other men. I began to see that it is just too much to ask a girl to ignore everybody but you. The only thing you can do is be the most attractive man you can and keep the relationship interesting and full of passion.

After Number Ten, I erased the key logger. I accepted women for what they were, and I didn't need to invade their privacy anymore to understand them. I saw that the key logger had ruined relationships for me. There were girls that would have given up everything if I would have just dived in head first and trusted them. There were also girls that wouldn't have given up anything, but now that I know I should expect it, I won't be caught off guard.

It has made me feel more like playing the field until I find the exact right girl is the right choice, because you can bet that she will be doing the same thing. The key logger opened my eyes to reality.

The reason I could finally delete the key logger is because I finally felt that I understood the other side of women, the side they want to hide. From these ten relationships and even more that I didn't write about, I had seen the big picture.

Everything went perfectly and a few months later, I met a girl I really liked. So many things about her were so right and things started getting serious between the two of us.

Months and months passed by and the relationship only got better. Up until this point I had hardly thought about the key logger, but as things had taken another step towards serious, I used the argument: "How can I make such a big commitment without knowing the truth."

I convinced myself. And, after so much time not using the key logger, I installed it once again. This time I installed a much simpler version, because I thought I only needed it for a small amount of time.

I used it to easily get her Facebook password and as I logged in, I waited for the dirt that I was always found.

It wasn't long before I saw it. A guy told her:

"I want to do it like we did it before." There were other things that pointed to her sleeping with this guy after we had already met.

"Not again. I wouldn't do that to my boyfriend." She replied to him.

It was all I needed to read. The next moment I saw her I told her if she wanted anything more with me she would give me her Facebook password right away. She accepted too easily.

As I looked through her messages she looked calm. Even as I clicked on the conversation she kept cool.

As I showed her the passages and all I remember is a blur of me yelling and her crying.

She used the following arguments over and over again:

"He's not from here and he's never been here. He was just a pen pal, then we started liking each other, but that was a long time ago."

And

"He was talking about us webcamming like before. I webcammed with him while I was in the breaking up stages with my ex."

I was barely listening and the night ended in her storming off an hour later. She had left her Facebook open telling me she had nothing to hide.

With my heart still pumping, I sat down and started carefully combing through her complete conversation with the guy. As I read, the things she told me started to make sense.

I checked his profile and I saw that he was Italian. From his collection of photos, it looked like he had never left his own country.

Then, I pretended to be her and threw in some questions about their past. Every single thing she told me checked out. The previous conversations with the guy matched up with what she had said.

I had been wrong and I completely overreacted. As I looked through her other conversations I began to see that this girl had been 100% faithful to me. She would barely respond to the army of guys that would flirt with her and rebuffed all advances.

I apologized to her, but something may have changed that day. We fought a lot for the next couple months and eventually broke up.

I went on with my life and the key logger I installed on my computer stayed there. I had forgotten about its existence and the key strokes it saved were untouched for the next few months. Then, I met a beautiful 19 year old girl.

Number Twelve – What a Sweet Heart

I was walking into the food court of a mall when a young girl caught my eye. From what I had learned about reading women's body language, I had caught hers as well. I saw that she liked me and I took it as an excuse to go to her table and start talking to her.

"Hi. I'm (my name)."

A huge smile crept over her face as I introduced myself and that is the best way to explain the progression of this relationship: like a smile creeping over a face.

We kept talking for the next few hours. Everything was going perfect and I asked her to come see a movie with me. She accepted and we got up from the food court table and started walking toward the cinema.

I stared at her as we walked. She was small with beautiful eyes. She was dressed in a way that wasn't overly slutty, but really made her features pop. She showed the right amount of cleavage and wore the perfect bra to show it off the right way.

Her pants and shirt were tight around her hips, showing her excellent, god given curves. This girl really knew how to dress to her body.

We kept talking and laughing, even through the movie. I'm sure the five or six other people in the empty movie theater got annoyed with us, but it didn't matter, we were in our own world.

It all seemed so natural that she would end up at my place.

As we were getting ready to have sex and I was about to put on the condom, I told her I didn't want to.

"Why not? We should use it." She said.

"Because I already know I'll be spending a lot of time with you. What's the difference between taking the chance now and taking it later if I already know I will be taking that chance with you?"

I had made a good case and I'm sure she felt the connection as well. I didn't wear a condom and the sex was… amazing.

We did it a couple more times before we both fell asleep in my bed.

Over the next few weeks we continued seeing each other. Whenever I had free time I would call her to see if we could meet up. She was surprisingly busy with school. I would try to see her some nights and she wouldn't be able to because of homework. However, when we planned a night to be together, she would always show up and right on time.

During pillow talk one night I asked her one of my normal questions:

"How many guys have you had sex with in your life?" Before I let her answer I went on adding "Most girls lie about this question. All I ask is that you are honest with me about it. I won't blame you for being with quite a few guys; after all, I HAVE been with quite a few girls."

"Three." She replied. "I'm only 19 years old, what kind of girl do you think I am?" I questioned her over and over again about it. The number seemed a bit low, but she insisted that it was the truth. I accepted it thinking "It doesn't really matter; I bet it's more like nine though."

We started seeing more and more of each other and everything was going perfect. Then one day as we were lying in bed she said

"My friend sent me the cutest picture on Facebook yesterday, you have to see it." Her phone was dead and she logged into her account from my computer. She showed me an adorable picture of her friends sleeping puppy lying on his back. She checked some of her messages and then logged out of her account.

We spent the rest of the night together and, as always, had amazing sex.

When I woke up the next morning she was gone. I turned on my computer and started surfing the internet when a thought popped into my head:

"You never un-installed the key logger… you can see what type of girl you have been dating."

I rejected the thought and went back to surfing the internet. I had the day free and I spent most of it on my computer. As each hour went by I got more and more curious. The familiar feeling of curiosity mixed with accessing something off limits was getting more and more powerful.

I finally gave in. I opened up the key logger and got her Facebook password.

I logged in and, thanks to a lot of experience searching Facebook accounts, went to the search function to search for certain keywords like: sex, cheat, (my name), fuck, etc.

When I searched sex, the amount of hits I got was astonishing. That word had been used hundreds of times. I checked out some of the conversations.

I opened one up and checked out the guy's timeline. He was older, in his early fifties. Why was she using that word with him? I went back to the conversation.

"Sex with you was amazing last night." He had said a few months earlier. My heart skipped a beat and I got a sick feeling in the pit of my stomach.

Was this her ex-boyfriend? As I read through the conversation I learned how wrong I was to assume that.

He had been paying her to sleep with him. Then, he had been paying her to help set up threesomes with her and another girl. She would get a nice commission from him and the amount of times they had done it was ridiculous.

I went to some of the other conversations and I noticed most of them were the same. Guys were paying her to have sex with them, a lot of them. But that would make her… a prostitute.

I had been dating a seemingly very successful prostitute. I thought back to all the times I had slept with her without a condom, completely unaware of what her real job was.

I started feeling even more sick at the thought of all the STD's I could have. I immediately called a doctor and set up an appointment. I called her too, telling her that we have to talk.

Before she arrived I thought up a bullshit excuse as to why we had to end it. I didn't want to confront her about it, I just wanted it over.

As I imagined how she would react, I thought back to some of the conversations I read on her Facebook. She would flirt with these guys that would buy her body, she would say she cared about them and loved to see them. She would say the same things over and over again, to each guy.

This made me imagine that she would react to the news that we were finished with a poker face; as unaffected as she would react if she lost a client.

The reality was a bit different. Tears ran down her face as she kept questioning why I didn't want to be with her anymore. After she lied to me about being a professional prostitute, why was I the one starting to feel guilty?

"We are drifting apart and I think it's better if we say goodbye now."

I will admit that her tears got to me, but it doesn't change the fact that this girl lied to me about being a hooker and let me sleep with her without any protection at all.

She had looked me in the eyes and swore to me that she had only slept with three men in her life. Wow… that seemed so ridiculous after learning the truth.

She seemed so sweet; I would have never guessed where she spent her nights when she wasn't with me. She would look me in the eye and tell me she was doing something, while in reality she was getting fucked by some old guy who had probably been with countless other prostitutes.

Then, she would return to my bed; pretending that she really was studying or going to class.

Is the key logger morally right?

Number Twelve had left me more confused than ever about the morality of the key logger. My serious relationship with Number Eleven had left me thinking that using a key logger was a terrible idea. But now, after what happened with Number Twelve, I had no idea what to think.

If I had never used the key logger on number twelve, who knows how serious I would have gotten with her before learning the truth. Maybe she would have gotten pregnant. Maybe I would have gotten AIDS. Who knows, I could have ended up marrying her, completely clueless to the manipulative nature of this girl.

If I never used the key logger, I never would have seen how she would pretend to genuinely like some of her clients and they would, seemingly, genuinely believe her. They would see her again and again, helping her bank account grow while she led them to believe that there was something more than a transaction between the two of them.

The last two girls I had used the key logger on had been so utterly different. One never deserved to be spied on. She had been a complete angel and deserved my complete trust.

The other had spent the entire relationship lying to me over and over again. She had cheated on me who knows how many times.

How could I have seen? Without the help of the key logger how could I have known that this girls entire job was based around making herself appear innocent. I couldn't have had any idea who she really was, could I?

I deleted the key logger after that, I still think it causes more harm than good. It poisons the trust in a relationship, which eventually leads to an implosion.

I can't sit here and tell you not to use a key logger, not with somebody that affects your life in such a personal and powerful way as your significant other, but I will tell you that even after what happened with Number Twelve, the prostitute, that I don't think a key logger is necessary. I have found that the key logger will bring bad things to the relationship every time you use it.

Learn from my knowledge and experiences and use them and take my advice for what it is… advice.

My advice is this: Understand that women aren't perfect, that they will do fucked up shit sometimes. Then, do your best to find that special girl that does those things the least and start building trust. Don't destroy that trust by installing a key logger.

Patterns

I was able to get a different point of view on women in a lot of relationships thanks to the key logger. Here are some of the patterns that I was able to see from all these experiences:

Multiple Men

Women are more naturally monogamous than men, but that doesn't mean that they are naturally monogamous. There are three types of men that women keep around in a romantic way: Orbiters, Serious Prospects, and Ex-Boyfriends.

Orbiters

An orbiter is a guy that a woman keeps around that she has no real attraction for or intention of dating. She keeps them around for validation, possible gifts, rebounds, and for somebody to talk to who is always there.

Validation - Women are naturally insecure, so having a guy that is in love with her is very beneficial. Every time a guy tells a girl she is pretty it makes her feel good about herself for a moment. If a guy tells her he is in love with her, she will feel good for even longer. She needs this in her life, the only problem is the more times she hears this from a particular guy, the less effect it will have. That is the reason why some girls will grow tired of orbiters after a while.

Possible Gifts - Women will also use orbiters to do things for them. This may be to take them to dinner, or if they are bored to take them to a movie. They could ask them to run errands for them. Women are not angels and their looks are their strongest weapon, it would be ridiculous not to expect them to use that weapon to improve their lives. One of the reasons I rarely buy things for women and don't always pay for dates is just this and I don't want to act like one of her many orbiters.

Rebounds - An orbiter is also the perfect rebound if she gets rejected or something else bad happens. Women are very emotional and one of the best ways of getting over the fact that a certain guy doesn't like her is to turn to another guy that is telling her how perfect she is. A woman will keep an orbiter around to soften the blow of another guy breaking her heart. In fact, about the only way an orbiter will actually get a shot with the girl is as a rebound. However, this makes it much harder to hang onto her after her feelings have returned back to normal.

Somebody to talk to - Women are also naturally very social and sometimes just want someone to listen. This can be surprisingly hard to find because of the fact that men, on average, just don't like talking as much. Women can use orbiters as listeners and because they are dangling the prospect of something more in front of the orbiters face, they will go out of their way to listen.

All orbiters are interested in the girl they are orbiting. Some orbiters have admitted their feelings and others have pretended to be just friends, but in every situation the girl has an idea of the orbiters feelings for her.

Serious Prospects

There are two types of serious projects: long term relationship prospects and pure attraction prospects.

Women see serious prospects in two ways; the first is as a future husband or boyfriend. They are attracted to these guys, but the reason they like these guys is because choosing them is more safe and logical. Passion will not be as high with these men.

The second type they are with because of pure attraction. Every time they see them they feel nothing but yearning and attraction. They don't believe that the guy will be faithful and commit, but they ignore this because they have such strong feelings. A girl who is with a guy that is higher value than her will usually have these feelings. These guys are usually the cause of cuckolding which I will talk more about later.

However, if you want to be the ultimate prospect, you want to fall into both categories. You don't want to be seen as a player, but you want to be seen as higher value than her.

A girl is at constant war with herself. She wants stability, but also passion. She wants to feel stronger emotions, but stronger emotions means work both ways, it means feeling amazing and feeling terrible. She wants the highest value possible guy, a guy who can have any girl he wants, but chooses not have to take them. She wants to believe that you have chosen only her, that you turned down prettier and higher value girls for her. To teach you how to be that man would take another book, but just understand that if you show those things well, any girl will fall in love with you.

Luckily, those prospects are about as rare as hitting the lottery for a woman, so you shouldn't feel bad if you can't master the two sides.

Once a girl has her serious prospects, it doesn't mean that she is ready to commit. She could be keeping them around in case they can't find something better. She might keep them around because she feels such strong attraction, but won't date them because she knows they will break her heart. It might be that those prospects aren't interested in more with her, but she is hanging onto the possibility.

Women may have three or four serious prospects. She may be trying to work it out with her first option, while keeping around the other serious prospects in case it doesn't work out.

It's important to know that a girl will always want to get the highest value man that she can. The reason that women cheat so much is that they find themselves in a relationship with a man they may even love, but when another guy that is higher value comes along, they want to give the higher value man a shot, without losing the guy they already have.

Ex-boyfriends

Ex-boyfriends are the ultimate baggage that a girl will carry. The longer the girl was with her ex-boyfriend, the more baggage that she will carry. Even if time has caused their old relationship to end, there will be feelings that may never go away.

If a girl has spent years talking to a guy every day, she will probably continue talking to him every day. Habits like that are not easily broken. Even if they have stopped seeing each other, it's very easy for a girl to be intimate with a guy even without it being physical. This can cause strong feelings. After she finds another guy, it's natural that the ex-boyfriend will feel jealousy. At this point he will usually try to play with her emotions to get her back.

They say ex-boyfriends are the guys that women are most likely to cheat with and for good reason. Any song or smell can trigger old emotions and if they are alone with each other when that happens, it's not too farfetched to imagine what can happen next.

Ex-boyfriends are one of the hardest things to deal with. You can tell her never to talk to him again, but eventually she will find a way. You can give her complete freedom and make it easy that they will find themselves in a situation when those feelings come back and they are alone. I believe the best course of action is somewhere in the middle. Boundaries, but don't expect them to totally cut off contact. Number Nine was not able to talk talking to her boyfriend and me telling her to stop talking to the guy she had dated for three years, was absolutely unreasonable.

Possible fallbacks and future options

A big reason that women have all these men around them is for possible fall backs and future options. If something doesn't work out with their number one option they want to keep open the possibility they can still have their second, third, and fourth options.

If she is dating a guy, but the whole relationship blows up, she wants somebody else to be able to turn to. If he cheats on her, she wants a high value guy to be able to turn to. Women know that nothing is certain, so they will keep other guys around to protect themselves. The problem is that when they start having feelings for one of these guys, they may start subconsciously sabotaging the relationship.

I can't tell you how many girls have given me their numbers when they had boyfriends. Of these women, there are some that will not give me the time of day because they are really loyal women. However, they still talk to me and flirt with me because of the possibility that their current relationship will end and they will be able to move onto another high value guy.

They gave me their number with no intention of cheating, but by doing this and flirting with me when we talked, they opened themselves to being seduced by me. It's not easy, but when a girl meets a future prospect she leaves a small window for herself to start developing emotions for him.

I have never met a committed girl who is completely closed to keeping contact with a guy as a future option. It's rare that a guy has the skill to turn that small window into the girl cheating, but of the hundreds of guys a girl meets a month those odds go up.

Every girl I key logged always left open the possibility for a high value guy to be a fall back or future prospect. The more loyal the girl, the smaller window they would give the guy and the higher value he must be to even get that window. But nonetheless, they would give the guy a window.

Monogamy vs. multiple men

I honestly believe every girl wants to be in a monogamous relationship, however, them not being monogamous stems from a combination of these four things:

1. They can't get a guy that lives up to their expectations

There are women that have been able to land a high value guy, after that, a guy like that becomes their expectation. Because it was a matter of luck that they obtained that guy or because their value has gone down since then, they will never find that guy again. They will play the field because they still have desires to be in a relationship, but they won't make a serious commitment because they still think they can get better.

2. A higher value guy comes along

People always want more, a better house, a better car, or even a better boyfriend or husband. You can fight human nature all you want, but those feelings will always be there, even in the most loyal of woman. They may sleep with two men, hoping the high value man will commit, while staying with her boyfriend in case he doesn't. The best way to combat that is to be the highest value guy that she could possibly attain.

To understand how to become a high value man, read my book *Understanding Sexual Attraction: What Makes a Woman Want You.*

3. Over time, people will grow bored of each other. Such is human nature.

It's a fact of life that the passion and strong feelings will dim with time. The stronger the original feelings the longer those strong feelings may stay, but eventually they will fade away.

What happens in long relationships is that it becomes a comfort of having that other person with you. After toughing it out for so long, people become dependent on each other, and the thought of facing life without the other person keeps the relationship strong.

However, when it is a couple that doesn't depend on each other and the only thing that kept them together were the strong feelings, after those feelings start to fade a woman might start to look for somebody else that she has those feelings with. If she starts looking, she will find it.

4. Women are sexually attracted to more than one guy, feelings aside.

Women may usually only have feelings of intense love for only one or two men at a time, but in a purely sexual sense, women are attracted to many guys. Variety is the spice of life, and women are not an exception to that piece of human nature.

Expect her to have many options

In every one of the 12 relationships that I went over, every single girl had more options than I originally expected. There was not one that had less than I expected. You would think after all that time, I would finally start guessing higher, but women are experts at making themselves look like they are less promiscuous than they really are.

Of the twelve relationships, once or twice they were as promiscuous as I originally perceived, but never were they less promiscuous. On top of that, 10 or 11 times out of 12, they were more promiscuous.

Women have learned that men don't see slutty girls as relationship prospects. This is because innocence is attractive, men want to be the experienced and dominant ones, and because men have learned that slutty girls are the type of girls that are guaranteed to break your heart. Because of this women will always do what they can to be perceived as less slutty than she already is.

If you meet a girl that appears slutty, you can pretty safely assume she is even sluttier than she appears. The same goes for the good girl. Every once in a while you may run into a virgin or a very religious girl. Even these girls are going to be more promiscuous than they appear, but usually more emotionally promiscuous than sexually.

I spent some time in a very Mormon college town. Having sex before marriage is VERY against the Mormon religion, but behind the veils you would hear whispers of "perfect Mormon girls" making mistakes.

I've never been to a place where it was easier to kiss a girl. Many of these girls will kiss a new guy multiple times a week. The same scandals of cheating happened there as anywhere else, only more often it was emotional cheating.

Even there, every girl I ever met and really got to know was more promiscuous and had more options than I expected.

The Age of Technology

We now live in an era of smartphones, social media, and texting. Never in the history of mankind has it been easier for women to be promiscuous without anybody finding out. The temptation is obvious and it is too easy for women to ignore. A girl without a smartphone or a Facebook is a girl that is much less likely to cheat than a girl with them.

On the other hand, these things have also made it much easier for men to cheat as well. The age of technology makes maintaining a successful marriage harder than ever.

Lies

Lies are something that everybody accepts as wrong. Lies are also something everybody should expect when dealing with women.

Not one woman that I have ever been with has ever gone a day without lying to me at least once, I guarantee it. In fact, just from what I found from my key logger, every girl I key logged has lied to me at least a couple times about something important, and those are just the lies I was able to find out.

The Rarest Truth

Because being promiscuous is so detrimental to a girl's chance at a future with a guy, you can pretty much expect that a girl will nearly almost lie about these questions:

How many guys have you slept with?

Of every single girl I key logged, I saw some sort of proof or at least a hinting that they lied to me about the number they told me. I honestly think the only girls that have been honest with me about this are the virgins and there have even been times when girls lied to me about being virgins like Number Five.

Every time I ask a girl how many guys they have been with I never accept their first answer and, after a while of saying it's impossible, they almost always say another number, usually about double their first answer. Even after that second number, it usually turns out that the number was even higher. Women have little reservations about lying partly because they have needed it to survive since the dawn of man.

There was a study I remember reading where they unanimously asked straight people from all over the world how many people they had had sex with in their lives. I remember that the average for men was about twice as high as the average for women. But think about it, it's an average, the numbers should match exactly. Even in a unanimous study, women could not tell the truth about how many people they had slept with (although there may have been exaggerations by men as well). If most girls couldn't tell the truth in a unanimous study, how could you expect them to tell the truth to somebody they see as a future prospect, when they know it could damage the relationship?

When was the last time you had sex?

This is the other one I believe women lied to me about 90% of the time. As always women want to be perceived as more innocent than they really are. They may even lie to themselves saying:

"Oh well, those guys never called me back, and I don't want to think about them so those don't count. I will just tell him when I had sex with my last boyfriend."

So they will only count their serious boyfriends. When you ask that question to a woman, you almost have to expect them to lie.

Lies don't destroy relationships, the truth does

That is how women think. Every single one of my twelve relationships never stood a chance because of the lies, but the only reason it ended up destroying the relationship is because I knew the truth.

If I would have never had a key logger, I'm positive that I would have had serious relationships with some of those girls. I would have never expected them to lie and maybe, with a more serious commitment, they would have been more faithful, but they would still lie.

This almost goes with the saying "ignorance is bliss." All girls will lie and when you find out they lie to you, it will kill the trust. Without trust, a relationship will never work. The only thing you can do is hope that she will only tell small lies that don't affect your relationship and just enjoy your time with her. She will hide things and lie to you and tell herself that it is all so you don't get hurt.

Why Women Lie

There are many reasons why women lie to men, but I will show you a few of the most common reasons.

Unreasonable societal expectations

Society has put unreasonable expectations on women. They are expected to look temptation in the eye every day on their smart phones and ignore it completely. Men look at women and expect them to not even think about other men, when that same guy is undressing every decent looking girl he sees in his mind.

Women have an expectation to be something that they are naturally not. Women have sex drives just like men. There are women with very high sex drives that are expected to stick to one guy that doesn't turn her on, something as amazing sex is not about to be ignored by anyone. You can't expect a girl like that to stay faithful to a guy that is giving her that.

If society was able to see these girls for what they needed then maybe a guy could enter an open relationship with her, or change himself to be more attractive to her. It's so much easier to lie and pretend she doesn't want more. It's easier to have a boyfriend and cheat on the side or to play the field, but admitting that this is her nature will only bring her problems.

To keep a prospect

Women feel like they need to have prospects around, they feel like they need to have their boyfriend or they need to have somebody to talk to in case things go wrong.

If a girl gets caught up in the moment and goes to see her ex-boyfriend, she will lie to her boyfriend because she feels she needs him. She usually won't even think of telling him the truth. If she doesn't have time to see one of her prospects very often and he asks her for her feelings so he can know if he should move on, she will lie to him and tell him that something could happen between them, because she feels she needs him, even if it's not as a boyfriend.

Women will not always lie in these situations, but when they feel like they NEED something, they will almost always lie to keep it.

Validation

Getting constant validation is something that women crave. She will drop any hints and lies about a potential relationship to a guy that makes her feel good about herself. She will tell him what he wants to believe so that he will continue validating her. As always though, there are exceptions and there are women that won't do this. If a woman is getting enough validation from her boyfriend, she won't feel the need to go searching for this.

Rationalization "I don't want to hurt him"

Women will lie to a guy because she doesn't want to "hurt" the guy. She will tell him she likes him because she doesn't want to make him feel bad. However, many times these are just ways to rationalize what she is really doing. By telling a guy a lie not to hurt him, she is postponing the eventual hurt and at the same time letting him waste his time on her; all things which are usually beneficial to him. In fact, it is usually only when she is bored of a guy that she will be completely honest with him, because then it is beneficial.

She absolutely convinces herself that she is lying to him for the right reasons, but in the back of her mind she knows it will end up worse, she just decides not to think about it.

Manipulation

For thousands of years women have been not been able to get what they wanted by physical force; they have been forced to learn how to get others to do their bidding. Over time this has made them very good at manipulating men. Women use lies to manipulate men into doing what they want. It's nothing except how nature has designed them.

Heartbreak Defense

A big reason women will be very deceptive is not because of any bad intentions, but because they are trying to cushion the blow of a broken heart. There are not many things as painful as a broken heart, for men and for women. Women will take all these steps to prevent it, that ultimately end up making relationships much more painful, but that is the world that we live in.

A shoulder to cry on

Every single girl that I had a longer relationship with from my twelve relationships had a shoulder to cry on when something went wrong.

I would constantly notice a pattern. If I didn't text a girl back for a day, she would go on a date with one of her orbiters. If I told her I wanted to know her better before committing she would tell another guy she loved him and missed him. She would do all these things as a sort of fall back for how she was feeling. It was completely deceptive and wrong, but she did it to feel better about herself.

As a guy who has done the exact same thing I can't blame women for it, but it is hard to believe how easily they do it; when the do this they are deceiving both men.

Backup plans

Women always try to have a backup plan. If she is starting to fall for you, she will also think back to a similar feeling she had with another guy and the pain that he caused her. So many times I could not understand how a girl that was falling for me could tell another guy "I miss you." Really it was her trying to put herself in a shielded position in case I broke her heart. She keeps them around for a backup plan so that if the guy they really like hurts them, they have somebody to soften the blow.

I have been both the backup plan and the guy they are worried will break their hearts. I used to think I was being slighted even as the guy they were worried would break their heart, when really the only guy getting slighted is the backup plan. As I have learned to not trust what women say, I also can't feel bad when they lie about their feelings to another guy because of how much they like me. It's the sad but ugly truth.

Commitment

The reason women look for a commitment with a guy they really like is because they want to feel safe in the relationship. The commitment turns into their "heartbreak defense", instead of the other men. If a woman lets the commitment be used like this and gets rid of her other prospects there is not a problem. The problem is that most women will keep them around even after starting a committed relationship.

Women Subconsciously Want the Best Possible Children

Women subconsciously are attracted to the highest value man; however, many times they cannot get this man to commit. In this situation some women will want the best from both worlds.

Cuckoldry

In my twelve relationships I witnessed attempted cuckoldry and talk about cuckoldry a few times. Cuckoldry is when a woman sleeps with a man and gets pregnant. She then tells another man that it is his child so he will raise and support that child.

It is very unlikely that a girl will end up with the exact man she wanted, however, it is much easier for a woman to sleep with a man than to get him to commit.

Subconsciously she wants this high value man's genetics to be passed along to her kids, but when the only way to do that is to deceive another man, it's a choice that is taken more times than you might imagine.

I believe cuckoldry is one of the most common, and most hidden things in society. A friend once told me that many hospitals know when a baby is not the child of the father, but they cannot tell him. I think if every man made sure that his kids were actually his, a fifth of the relationships on the world would be rocked. All I have to prove this is what I have seen of women when nobody is looking, but it is my opinion it is unbelievably common that a man is raising another man's child without any knowledge of it.

Genetics

It is simple survival theory that women want to pass on the best possible genetics to their offspring. Women feel this desire and when they can't fulfill it in an honest way; many will do it in an un-honest way. It is so important and drilled into them that scheming to get their ideal man turn into an "ends justify the means" situation.

Provider love vs. passionate love

A woman loves a guy who takes care of her kids in a different way. The sex will never be as good and the emotions so strong, but she will feel safe and taken care of.

She will look at a high value guy with a connection in another way. She will stop being so careful, even if she knows the chances are good they won't end up together. She knows he has very good genetics even if it's clear he has been with many women. High value men have options and subconsciously she wants her children to be high value and have options as well.

What to Look For

You have learned all this information about women, but it hasn't offered many solutions on how to find the right one. I have spent a lot of time looking for the right girl and I will share with you how you can find her too. These are not rules and by no means should be treated as such, but they can save you a lot of heart ache.

Exceptions

I want to start by saying there are exceptions to every rule. There IS a girl out there that never lies about important things. There IS a girl out there who will never give another guy a shot at her if you commit. However, you must accept that finding those girls is very difficult. The only thing you can do is get close and hope you will be able to see positive signals of her loyalty.

Attraction factor

Before you dream about your super model wife understand that the more attractive the girl, the more options she will have to get a higher value man than you. I personally can't date a girl I'm not attracted to and you shouldn't, but you shouldn't not give a girl a shot at a long term relationship just because she's not the most attractive girl you have dated. Long term relationships are more about her personality than her looks anyways.

Your value in comparison to hers

A woman will always want the highest value man possible. If you are dating a girl that is higher value than you, she will constantly be looking for reasons why she chose you when she can logically get higher value. You can spend the whole relationship proving what you have to offer, or you can date a girl will lower sexual value than you. In relationships there is nearly always somebody that dates down.

The virgin

The ultimate long term relationship prospect is the same as it has been for thousands of years, the virgin. Every virgin I have slept with, has instantly fallen in love with me. It has gotten to the point that I WILL NOT sleep with a virgin unless I feel very strong feelings towards her. A girl who knows no other men will not feel the same desire to be with other men that a girl who has already been with many men.

Along with this there is a romantic aspect to taking a girl's virginity. Attractive girls that save their virginity usually do it for a reason; they want to save it for that special guy. By doing this they show self-control and loyalty. They are the ultimate long term relationship prospect if you want trust. But beware, women know this as well and it's the reason so many women lie about it.

The best girls for long term relationships are the girls that have long term relationships

If a girl has only been in long term relationships, there is usually a reason. She feels a need to be with a guy, she is also most likely loyal, or those relationships would have had a better chance of ending sooner. There is also an art to knowing how to have a long term relationship and these girls will be the best at it.

Avoid the slut

Any guy who has spent some time dating has probably learned one of the most important rules: Don't fall for a slut.

The slut has a high sex drive and has become accustomed to being with many men. It is possible to keep her loyal for a period of time with great game, but for a long time I wouldn't count on it.

The slut is even better at cheating because she has had more practice. It will be much harder to catch her in the act, but she will ultimately do it. There is nothing wrong with having a relationship with a slut, as long as you accept then and there that she is eventually going to cheat on you. If you don't, you are in for a lot of emotional pain.

How to Improve Your Relationship

When I learned all this information there were points when I honestly believed that women's deceptive nature meant that I could never have a good long term relationship. With time I learned that I had to accept women as they are and not expect more of them than they could give.

Don't be needy

This is one of the principal rules in building attraction with a girl and it is just as important in long term relationships. One of the ultimate forms of neediness is jealousy.

When you are jealous you are subconsciously saying, "I am not confident that I am the highest value man that you have access to." You are basically admitting that there are better options to her than you, or at least, that is how she will interpret it subconsciously.

You should give a girl her freedom. Don't tell her never to talk to her ex-boyfriend; don't forbid her to go out with her friends. Show that you are confident that you are the highest value man that she can have and it will make you more attractive.

However, there is a balance here. You should still make rules. You should not forbid your wife from talking to her ex-boyfriend but you should not let him be intimate with him or let her be alone with him in a private place. You can let her go out with her friends, but if she flirts with another guy while you are there she is disrespecting you and you should act. Punish her in any way. If you have to, you should leave her, because letting her walk all over you will change how she sees you and kill the relationship anyways.

Ignore minor lies and give leeway

As I have mentioned many times, girls will lie. You can't be paranoid and always wondering about when she is lying. You must accept that she will lie, but be confident that you have chosen a girl that would not lie to you about something very important. It can be very difficult to ignore lies and there are times when it is the RIGHT thing to do to call her out on a lie. You just want to make sure that you call her out on a lie that is a betrayal, like seeing a handsome friend in a date-like atmosphere, rather than on something small like where she was at 2pm (when she was at her favorite clothing store that she knows you can't afford, so she doesn't mention it).

As I have mentioned, girls don't think like men. Their word doesn't hold the same value. It is literally how they are genetically engineered so, as I have said many times, accept it.

If you want a relationship to work, sometimes you have to choose between your pride and the relationship. She is going to do shady things and she is going to lie. Every man will put up with a different amount. If she completely betrays you, you should leave her, but if you freak out about every little lie it can eat away at a good relationship.

The truth is, you cannot trust women… but you must.

Final Words

When I think back to using the key logger, I remember the feeling I had when I logged into their accounts. It was a mix of sickness and excitement, guilt and curiosity. Because of all the emotions I felt for these girls, just thinking of the key logger would make my stomach feel sick. I do not suggest using a key logger to anyone reading this book; it will lead to some of the hardest truths you will ever have to face. It's better to learn from my experiences and take what you know into your relationship.

However, if you do decide to do this to someone you care about, I can only express my sentiments because you will find things that you did not expect.

When it comes down to it, the women that you see every day are not as they appear. The world and society has made them hide the truth because it is so hard to accept. For some reason the dark nature of women has been kept well… in the dark.

I believe that the best thing that could happen is that the hidden nature of women becomes public knowledge. I want this to happen so that the little boys who grow up dreaming of the true love they saw in a movie will not expect the impossible; so that the men who fall deeply in love with a girl won't destroy a relationship just because she lied to him one time.

Knowing this information could push men to do many things. It could push men to become players and forget serious relationships, to ignore the lies and deceits and pretend that everything is perfect, or to accept women as they are and do what they can to find the best of them. Whatever you choose to do with this information, just understand that this book is not about bashing the nature of women, only understanding it and accepting it.

I don't think lying is ok, but when it comes down to it, men and women are different: we are wired to think differently. Men may not lie as much or be as deceptive, but we are at times emotionally cold and not nearly as nurturing. The world is not black and white even if that's how people want to see it.

I could write a book about the dark nature of men. I would have plenty of material, but when it comes down to it, when you peak behind the curtain, nobody is really innocent.

About the Author

Nicholas Jack is a world traveler and student of women. He is never in one place for more than a few months. He enjoys learning and experiencing new things. He has written eight books.

www.ingramcontent.com/pod-product-compliance
Lightning Source LLC
Chambersburg PA
CBHW070554290526
45790CB00002B/687